I0453148

Dear Adultery

A Wife's Diary

tographed Especially For You!

Dear Adultery

A Wife's Diary

by Toni L. Garner

Dear Adultery
by Toni L. Garner

Published by:
UPH. Div., Maximized Productions, LLC.
6715 Suitland Road
Morningside, Maryland 20746
(701)484-3303
www.maximizedproductions.com/publishing/

Design Director: Dawn Harvey-Owens

Copyright © 2024 Toni L. Garner
All rights reserved
Library of Congress Cataloging-in-Publication Data:
Garner, Toni L
Dear Adultery / Toni L. Garner

ISBN: 979-8-9875001-8-7

Printed in the USA

Dedication

To God, we thank you for saving both of us. And to our family and friends, we thank you for loving us through it all.

Preface

"Why did Moses' command to give a bill of divorcement and to put her away? He saith unto them because your hardness of heart, Moses allowed you to divorce but from the beginning it was not" (Mathew 19:8).

Believing in the world is our weakness but believing in Prayer is our Strength. Jesus instructed, "Therefore I tell you, whatever you ask for in prayer, believe that you have received it, and it will be yours (Mark 11:24).

Table of Contents

Chapter One

How I Know Adultery

Summer 2021

This book is written with honesty and vulnerability. I am a woman who had a Christian foundation but found myself lost in a worldly dilemma. My problem, I was reading the Bible, but I was not living the Bible. I started a prayer wall but never followed through. A prayer wall is a quiet and private place (closet, car, etc.) with God where you write down your needs, wants, have discussions, worship, and sometimes go to battle against dilemmas. I devalued one of God's most precious gifts, prayer. "In everything you do, put God first, and He will direct you and crown your efforts with success," (Proverbs 3:6). Without Him, my marriage became a soap opera, my very own Love and marriage reality show. And when things fell apart, I read the Bible to prepare for my upcoming divorce. How pitiful is that? I did not read the Bible to gain strength, encouragement, or to reclaim my worth as a wife to save one of the most valuable gifts in life, my 'better half.' You know, the spouse I married and shared wedding vows with: "For better, for worse, for richer, for poorer, in sickness and in health, until death do us part. I will love and honor you all the days of my life." The trauma I experienced with the dramatics of my marriage, caused me to think God was preparing me for the divorce I was seeking, but He had something totally different in mind. This adulterous spirit came into my marriage bold, beautiful, full of promise. She came so confident, it was as if she looked at me like, "Winch, please, I got him. His flesh is his weakness and I do not need a college degree to graduate to this level of sin."

What this spirit did not realize is that God would use this attack on my marriage to position me to author this book, a tool against the enemy's attack on

> **Side Bar**
> "I need You every hour, every minute. I'm nothing without Your grace. Here I am, here I am Lord."
> Holy Water by We the Kingdom & Tasha Cobbs Leonard

marriage. Once again, proving God is victorious. Know that I am sharing the most intimate part of my marriage because of

God. He wanted me to put Him first. He wanted me to regenerate family by overcoming one of marriages biggest destroyers, adultery. Like internet gossip, I want this diary to go viral. God wants His word spread in abundance like crops in the field. As in Matthew 13:1-9: 'The story of the Sower (someone who proclaims God's word) who scattered seeds (Gospel) in the soil across the land and depending on where the seeds landed on the ground (how a person perceives the Gospel), crops grew differently. The seeds that fell along the path were eaten by the birds (not spiritually engraved in the soul); the seeds that fell on rocky ground did not survive without the deep-rooted soil (a surface follower with no deep connection to God); those that fell on the thorns, grew but were choked by the thorns (easily dismayed by the world). But seeds that fell on good soil, produced crops in several large quantities (spreading God's word in abundance).' I am good soil, a willing participant in God's plan to spread His word but I did not start out this way.

I should have addressed adultery a long time ago when my marriage was at its weakest. I know as a woman, wife, and mother some of the shenanigans I discuss in this testimony is a direct result of not taking full advantage of the power of prayer. Through this testimony, I found my purpose in God's plan, to share the significance of prayer. Prayer does not stop havoc; it counters havoc through faith in Jesus. Eight years into our marriage, my husband decided to confess his encounter with adultery that took place during the first two years of our marriage. Before I had a chance to address this first offense or have the time to process the feelings of sadness, hurt, and anger, our marriage faced something even more traumatic, the suicide of my nineteen-year-old-stepson. Our seven-year-old son was the only one that had the right antidote for this type of pain. Because right after we told him the devastating news of his brother's death, he asked, "If we pray really hard, can God bring my brother back?" He knew who to go to and how to get to Him at such a young age, while we relied on our own recognizance. Suicide was so

14

catastrophic; we were emotional escape artist which became the platform of our marriage. This trauma relinquished us both from addressing adultery. Instead, she hid in secrecy, peaking around the corner and stayed concealed in the shadows for the next trespass. This one avoidance was so advantageous for adultery, she was like the spirit of Jezebel who was "a teacher of false prophetess while seducing servants to commit fortification and to eat things sacrificed to idols," (Revelations 2:20). This means she represented a life far from God's word and belittled God's purpose of marriage. Adultery is so accepted by the world; she has desensitized her destructive behavior and normalized her presence in marriage.

I could not get ahead of this hideous spirit because I was suffering from spiritual malfunction. I was stuck between Faithless Forgiveness vs. Faithful Forgiveness. Faithless Forgiveness - forgiving with the flesh which lingers in distrust vs. Faithful Forgiveness - forgiving through God and laying everything at his feet. As long as I lingered, I could not fight adultery. I let her become bigger than God. I let her become more important than me, the wife. I was letting her win, not in the way of winning or losing a competition because no one wins in sin. I mean in the way of giving adultery the power to destroy. I allowed her to make me feel small, discouraged, and useless as a wife. "Do not merely listen to the word, and so deceive yourselves. Do what it says. Anyone who listens to the word but does not do what it says is like someone who looks at his face in a mirror and, after looking at himself, goes away and immediately forgets what he looks like" (James 1:22-24). Without a relationship with God, I did not have the discernment to know her conviction was already set in the Ten Commandments, 'I shalt not commit adultery,' a testament already backed by God. A battle already destined with victory.

Adultery festered with time and showed up several years later. This time she came on a day that I was preparing to meet my husband for a Mother's Day event. I was feeling beautiful from the extra care I took with my hair, make-up, and dress to add some spice to my husband's day. Before I could walk out the door, adultery appeared with a vengeance, out of nowhere.

The details of how adultery appeared is not what this testimony is about. This testimony is to show what can happen in a marriage without God. This book is an antagonist to the adulterous spirit whose purpose is to destroy with distrust, betrayal, and retaliation of what God puts together. I barely remember driving to the event. The "I feel beautiful" moment was terminated in adultery's disgrace. To be honest, it was shocking like a death in the family, as if my better half was in an accident and suddenly died. Adultery drew a line straight down the middle of our lives causing us to become victims in our own marriage. Friends took sides built off our emotions. I told one friend and she cried, and another had tears in her eyes. One of the great things about marriage, it builds a village so one death touches everyone's life. We separated and lived in different houses and hired lawyers. Even after marriage counseling and reconciliation, it was never the same for me. And for my husband, he went back to what was familiar, his flesh. "Trust in Jehovah with all your heart and lean not upon thine own understanding. In all thy ways acknowledge Him and he will direct thy paths" (Proverbs 3:5). Instead, we controlled our marriage as if we were center stage, so the light did not shine on Him; and for that we suffered.

We did not just suffer because of my husband's sin, but mine as well. You see, my attempt at forgiveness conflicted with my faith. Faithlessness put me and my husband in a therapy session explaining to my son that we were divorcing. My lowest moment was seeing my son cry at a time when he should have been living his best childhood life instead of suffering in the aftermath of adultery. I struggled with forgiveness based on my own fears and uncertainties. Things felt so unreal. I remember one of the marriage counselors asked me, "So you took this deeply?" And I said yes. I remember thinking, "Should I take it some other way?" I honestly thought the suicide was more than enough to happen to any family. So, hadn't enough happened to mine? I figured since we met the 'terrible quota,' bad things would skip right over our house. But life soon displayed that's not possible, terrible is unavoidable. Because terrible can come at any time and to anyone in this sin filled world, no one is exempt from suffrage. And because we did not become one flesh as the Bible instructs, we were easily divided, opening our marriage to more devastation.

I think separation and divorce has a lot to do with fear and misconceptions. In the Bible, John 11:47, think of the chief priest and Pharisees who condemned Jesus. These men feared that Jesus would be their downfall because He was/is the Messiah; making the men feel inferior. Fear crucified Jesus and turned a few of His disciples against Him, because they were afraid of the outcome. The devil loves fear. Divorce is built off the same deception, as we look at the other spouse as our downfall, as they appear to easily crucify the marriage, fear creeps in. Fear of the unknown is living with a spouse every day, afraid they may be detrimental to your happiness, forcing you into survival mode. Fear brought thoughts that threatened our marriage; diminished our intimacy, devalued my husband as head of household, and demeaned my position as his help mate, and ultimately lead us astray.

The devil loves the non-adulterous spouse too because they become his weapon of revenge. I was gardening between the seeds not rooted in deep soil vs those that fell on the thorns and grew but were choked. I wanted my soon-to-be-ex to feel my pain and learn from it but that was never my place. We all answer to God, it was not for me to intercept God's hand or judgement. But I could not get past how the kids saw me, if I stayed in the marriage. Would they respect me? What kind of husband will my son be? How do I look at myself in the mirror? Where do I go from here? In trying to find peace in all of these questions, I began doing things to get to know myself, to master the part of me I lost. I looked for diverse ways to reestablish the view I had of myself. I found therapy in voice lessons and my teacher gifted me a listening ear in more ways than one. Suggesting lyrics close to my heart and soft off my lips.

Side Bar
"I don't get no sleep. I don't get no peace."

Girl Crush by Little Big Town

A healthy outlet for my soul, learning myself, while trying to find direction.

(1) *Prayer Wall: God, I don't know how to do this.*

Chapter Two

The Testimony

Voice therapy gave me confidence to say and feel what I needed, but best of all I was learning to worship God through my own voice. This is a huge piece and is truly instrumental in why I can write this book and the purpose of the side bars. It is important to show how words matter, no matter how they come out of your mouth or go into your heart. What you take in is what you put out, Amen. During our separation, I read the Bible more than ever. What is interesting about this is what I shared in the beginning. It was not because I was seeking reconciliation. I had no hope of recovering my marriage so I was reading the Bible more to be strong for the divorce. Not realizing this was the way God was preparing me to rely on the Holy Spirit. And the more I read the more I saw God showing me who I was without Him, and who I could become with Him. "Then you will call on me and come and pray to me, and I will listen to you. You will seek me and find me when you seek me with all your heart (Jeremiah 29:11-15)."

The day this testimony started; I was at my son's last therapy session. "He does not get a pass," for his behavior, the therapist explained, while she looked me straight in the eyes. In other words, he does not get to sweep bad behavior under the rug because he cannot deal with his own reality. I could see the therapist was not tolerant of my feelings as she saw the

guilt in my eyes from the damage me and my soon-to-be-ex, caused my son. The therapist was right; if our son does not get a pass, adultery should not and neither should this marriage. And just like that my journey to this testimony began. I called my 'soon-to-be-ex' and yelled at the top of my lungs, "You do not get a pass from the path of destruction you caused this family!" This was the beginning of how adultery met forgiveness and how hurt met healing. I was so relieved when the two met, it relinquished me of the emotional distress, I forfeited to release long ago. I would not have known the significance of this moment, if I did not spend all those months reading the Bible.

So, for the second time when a friend told me about his battle with adultery, I could finally hear his words. He told me his story a year earlier before I was ready and able to accept my own reality. This testimony is God's purpose for me; to save one of God's valued gifts, marriage. On this day, my ears were open to someone else's battle with adultery. A prime example of putting God first and spreading his seed.

My friend explained: He and his wife separated for two-years under adulterous circumstances. Two Years! My friend was doing everything in his power to get his wife and family back together. Until one day, he was talking to his brother, and he explained how he wanted his wife and family back so badly. The brother explained, "If God is pulling one of her arms and the devil is pulling the other, what do you think you are doing?" From that day, my friend said he just "stopped." He let God do His work and left his wife in His Hands. "For the husband is the head of the wife, as Christ is also the head of the church, being himself the Savior" (Ephesians5). Sometime, thereafter, his wife on her own accord with God's help, made her own decision to return to her family. He said it was hard in the beginning; Christian Counseling made them both look at themselves. Ten plus years later, they are still married, happily. My friend told me "You have to make God the center of your marriage." In Jeremiah 29:11-15, "For I know the plans I have for you," declared the Lord, 'plans to prosper you and not to harm you, plans to give you hope and a future." As I look back to that moment in the therapist's office, I know the Holy Spirit talked to me that day. I did not leave the same way I came in and I never looked back. I believe the conversation with my friend validated God's plan for me. I had sudden hope in an unknown future.

After the day I yelled to the top of my lungs, we began to talk more each day resulting in the decision to save our marriage. "For by grace have ye been saved through faith; and that not of yourselves, it is the gift of God," (Ephesians 2:8). I was in a dark place prior to this testimony, not realizing all I had to do is give it to God. I did not know how to save us since there is no light without Him. I did not know the true purpose of healing is the induction to having faith in prayer. My 'soon to be ex' was thirty days into his two-month business trip, six hours away by plane from where we lived. I decided my son and I were going to visit his father. The day of our flight, my son explained, "Mom, I do not know why I am telling you this but when my cousin was here (three months earlier), daddy went out one night and said he had an emergency at work." I do not remember giving my son too much of a reaction, but I knew he was the messenger. Because, several months before this trip, he asked me out of nowhere, "Do I have faith?" I asked him why he said that, and he could not give an answer. There was no turning back now. The fact that I was reading the Bible to find some kind of peace in divorce but redirected by the Holy Spirit to defy what adultery tried to communize, confirms His mighty power. I was not about to disregard or take this moment for granted. I quickly learned a formula in mastering faith in prayer because I did not want to be deaf to the Holy Spirit: Human Conflict needs Prayer to Understand Biblical Instruction as you are reading His Word, then this Rationalizes the Flesh to Know Discernment, resulting in Hearing the Holy Spirit (HC + P + UBI(HW)/RF + KD = HHS). Without the Holy Spirit, I could not have found the fire to 'wife-up.'

When my husband arrived to pick us up from the airport, I felt something I had not felt for a long time, safe again. Not the 'safe' you feel with the alarm on your house but the 'safe' a woman feels the day she decides 'he is the one.' On this trip, we enjoyed our family time as if history were erased. My husband and I started peeling off the band aids from the wounds of our marriage. This went well with the family intervention I planned that included the kids. During the intervention, I provided a general overview of our families' history and I remember my daughter (she was on FaceTime) saying, "Dad, you do not have to do this, if you do not want to." A statement from a true intervention. This same night, we sat in the bathroom for privacy, and I told my husband, "I came to save you." I do not mean that I am God, and it was my job to save him. For the sake of context, what I mean is that God instructed me to stay in position. As in, I was not to leave my post as his helpmate, his wife. The Bible says, "Likewise, wives, be subject to your own husbands, so that even if some do not obey the word, they may be won without a word by the conduct of their wives, when they see your respectful and pure conduct" (1Peter 3). Basically, if the husband loses his way to the flesh, the wife can lead, not through nagging and complaining but through her faithfulness in God. To this day, my husband referred to this moment as the parable of the drowning man, explained here.

The Drowning Man (author unknown)

A man was trapped in his house during a flood. He began praying to God to rescue him. Had a vision in his head of God's hand reaching down from heaven and lifting him to safety. The water started to rise in his house. His neighbor urged him to leave with him in his truck and the man said "no,' he was waiting for God to save him. Next, some people came in a boat and offered him a ride on the way to safety and again the man said "no," he was waiting for God to save him. Then a helicopter came over his home with the ability to lower a ladder to save him, and again the man waved the helicopter away, waiting on God to save him. Of course, he drowned and when he arrived in heaven, he asked God, "Why didn't you save me?" God replied, "I sent a truck, a boat, and a helicopter and you refused all of them. "What else can I possibly do for you?"

We have our own delusional expectations of our Savior. In marriage, we do the same by having unrealistic expectations of a spouse. Trapped in our own minds, our own version of marriage, and our own community we listen to, so we miss God's rescue mission.

During the visit, there were plenty of truths that came out in the open. This included when I looked through my husband's phone, leading him to admit he was not alone on this trip. Adultery surpassed my understanding of the destruction she can cause in marriage. I had to leave behind all doubts of faithless forgiveness as my son and I returned home several days later. I did not know what to do but we decided we were 'all in' before I got on the plane, so I knew to stay in position. One of the first things I did on my return home was send my husband and this woman a religious text based off a Christian song I was listening to repeatedly. The lyrics and quietest part of the song I would replay for my peace of mind were "I need You every hour, every moment. I'm nothing without Your grace. Here I am, here I am, Lord." I believed in these words. I was laying everything at His feet, and to this day, I listen to this song in tears remembering how far I have come in Jesus.

I am not sure what I expected in return, but she responded with some legal jargon explaining 'I should stop harassing my husband (His name was here) about her or some legal action will be taken against me; and I should respond to her legal jargon that I agree to these terms.' This was the last time I initiated communication with her, and I blocked her number from communicating with me. However, I explained to my husband, he is on dangerous ground because he continues to violate our marriage with her presence. He agreed to put this woman on a flight back home. My husband did not realize I had access (I told him later) to his email through a laptop we shared. Within 24 hours, I could see her flight was confirmed and then cancelled. I also read a chat between my husband and someone on his Facebook that explained, "She said she is not leaving, and she is driving back with me and what you tell your wife is between you and your wife." I asked him the next morning if she was leaving and he said "no" and he explained, he purchased the ticket, but she refused to leave. I said, "Let her know, she is welcome to stay but we will all ride back together." I do not know what my husband said to that woman, but she returned home on that same cancelled flight. All the glory goes to God, and this is what you must focus on as you read this testimony. It was never about me or us; it was/is about Him and what He will do through the power of prayer. "In their hearts humans plan their course, but the Lord establishes their steps" (Proverbs 16:9 NIV).

I do not remember when I got serious about my prayer wall, but I started one like the one in the movie War Room. I picked up that prayer wall I left behind and connected it to those gospel words like I was at war, and I became Gangsta when I wifed-up. In Acts 1:6-8, "And He said unto them, it is not for you to know times or seasons, which the Father hath set within His own authority. But ye shall receive power when the Holy Spirit is come upon you." This season of my life became my interpretation of the Roman Law I learned about in my Blue Letter Bible studies. A Roman Soldier could make a person from the cities they conquered carry their bags for one mile and only one mile. Matthew 5:41 writes about Jesus'

Sermon on the Mount which references a parable in relation to the Roman Soldier, "Whoever compels you to go one mile, go with him two." Jesus wants us to do more than expected for our marriages because He has done this for us by dying on the cross. If an adulterous spirit lurks into your marriage, going the extra mile is not just for the person who must find a place within themselves to forgive; but for those considering or acting in adultery must find a place within themselves to prohibit their own indiscretions.

Several days later, I received a call from my husband's phone number and the first thing the person said, in a very nasty tone was, "Do you EVEN know WHAT you want?" I asked, "Who is this?" She said, "You KNOW WHO THIS is." I responded, "You have the wrong number," and I hung up. I could feel my heart race, not in anger but because this type of conflict was not who I was. I questioned my husband and he confirmed she was no longer with him. I searched the internet to find an explanation of the call coming from my husband's number and found the technique of spoofing. The practice of falsifying the information of an incoming call on the receiver's caller ID display. The internet explained, it is legal in the United States unless done with the intent to defraud, cause harm, or wrongfully obtain anything of value. This was a perfect replication of adultery, defraud (lies), causes harm (destroys families), and wrongfully obtains anything of value (your spouse). The spirit of Adultery does not come in peace; and I knew not to engage in anything that stripped me from God's grace. "Put on the full armor of God, so that you can take your stand against the Devil's schemes" (Ephesians 6:11 NIV). Get familiar with God's line of defense because it is not of this world. His defense is meek as described by the "Ancient Greek, meekness is a person who is not passive or easily pushed around but strength under control. A strong stallion that was trained to do the job instead of running wild."

(2) Prayer Wall: God, please help my husband save our marriage.

The reason this woman is a big part of my testimony, is because she became part of God's lesson plan for me to pray

34

faithfully. God used something that our (me and my husband) flesh destroyed (marriage) to provide a spiritual growth spurt in the planting of His word. "For we wrestle not against flesh and blood, but against principalities, against powers, against the rulers of the darkness of this world, against spiritual wickedness in high places," (Ephesians 6). I knew I was in a spiritual and earthly battle from my new overwhelming faith in God, based on the center of the affliction, sin. The devil works through people, and our flesh is enticed by his faulty desires. I knew not to be a puppet dangling from his string and participating in any scene involving the devil's desires. In Timothy 3:1-5, he warns us of the characteristics of the last days, and I noted a few descriptions from the verse - without love, unforgiving, slanderous, without self-control, lovers of pleasure rather than lovers of God, and it ends by warning, "Have nothing to do with such people."

(3) *Prayer Wall: God is working. My husband "saw me," by admitting, he put me in this situation, backed me in a corner." God is smiling on my husband. Amen*

Chapter Three

Putting God First

The time came for my husband's return home. This meant we would live under the same roof after one-year and four months. Of course, things did not fall into place as if we were portraying a thirty minute 'Bill Cosby Show.' It was more like, 'As the World Turns;' a soap opera easily recalled ten years later. I called this the adaptation (arguing) period. I remember standing in the garage soon after my husband's return, and I told him to let this woman know, "I am going to fight for my family but not the world's way, but through prayer." Adultery and unforgiveness made our beds and now we had to lie down in it. "Set your mind on the things that are above, not the things that are above the earth" (Colossians 3:2). We were not quite ready for this frame of mind. The return home was between terrible and worse. We were still in the past with behaviors bound to idolatry as described in Colossians 3:5-8. This references misbehaviors that brings the wrath of God - fornication, uncleanness, anger, and shameful speaking out of your mouth. We broke the very first commandment, Exodus 20:3, "Thou shalt have no other gods before me." We were working backwards. We made our individual feelings more important than working within the Holy Spirit, again exasperating sin.

In all, we went through two separations with different lawyers each time, dragging our family and friends through it as well. During the last separation, we were in the middle of moving to another state, where we ended up living in the same neighborhood, 13 houses down from each other. This forced us to go through COVID together, which caused our initial divorce court date to be moved two months out which resulted in this testimony. And here we are back together again not making God center stage all over again.

One time I was asked why I separated from my husband initially, instead of staying to work it out. Honestly, at that time I did not know what to do but I knew I wanted to be as far as possible from the hurt and the cause. I had to account for myself and my own emotional state of mind and for me in my situation, we could not do it together. I believe to this day, if it was not for my, what I now call, sabbatical, I would not know God as I do today. The separation taught me the true power of prayer and was the addendum to my healing so I could save me to save us. For me, the sabbatical applied Psalms 23:3, "He restores my soul," to spiritual health and repairs injuries caused by the flesh.

During the adaption period, I learned forgiveness in marriage starts with setting boundaries for each other. These boundaries supply limits. The Internet defines limit as a boundary or point where something ends, or the maximum amount allowed. Boundary is the dividing line, limit, or location between two areas; while limit is a restriction, a boundary beyond which one may not go. Our marriage crossed boundaries and left no set limits; and reached the maximum amount allowed. The marriage was hard to rebuild but marriage counseling helped set the stage. One counseling session was challenging and ended like an upcoming divorce.

"A wise man will hear and increase learning, and a man of understanding will attain wise counsel" *(Proverbs 1:5).*

(4) Prayer Wall: I will not kick my husband out of the house. He can make his own decisions because God has given him that freedom. Amen

I reached out to the same friend who noted "You have to make God the center of your marriage." In frustration, I explained to him how my husband was reacting to discussions in our sessions. He shook his head and repeated the story regarding his marriage, and I said, "What did you mean by putting God in the center of our marriage? I thought I was doing that." He explained in so many words; 'YOU must learn to be quiet. Everything YOU think and feel does not need to be said. YOU must work on yourself because YOU have no control over the other person.' Through this phase of our marriage, I learned 1 Corinthians 13:4-5 NKJV, "[4] Love suffers long *and* is kind; love does not envy; love does not parade itself, is not puffed up; does not behave rudely, does not seek its own, is not provoked, thinks no evil." I want to share what resonated with me the most when I researched this scripture and found Love explained this way. To my understanding, love acts out loud with truth and patience; and does not compromise itself with nonsense due to emotional distress. Love is action that is practiced, matured, and graduated just like that stallion. Love, the last thing I expected to save my marriage but should have been the first.

Marriage counselling was a struggle for me not just because of the specific session I mentioned above. In my recollection, it seemed the counselor was almost accommodating every word or joke my husband expressed (now rolling my eyes). I had so much anxiety that I started to loath these sessions but for some reason, I felt it was not about me. I felt my husband needed to connect with the therapist. He needed an advocate. When I look back now, I realize I did not need quite the same support. I had to stay intentional with where my faith stood to continue to mature in the Holy Spirit. I know this will sound strange but in all this, I feel God made me walk in each person's shoes that played a part in this testimony. I saw my husband, myself, and this adulterous spirit to get an idea of their perspectives so I could learn how to reflect before I responded. "Bless those who persecute you; bless and do not curse," (Romans 12:14 NIV). This is a hard pill to swallow, but it is the only way to move forward. I was totally alone during this testimony. No family or friend's opinions played a role, no one knew about the six-hour flight, or the phone calls until I could be fully accountable for my own spiritual well-being. I stayed 'prayed up,' and this is how I refocused.

Several months later, again the woman called using my husband's number. This time she introduced herself and asked me not to put her on speakerphone. She did most of the talking and explained when she met my husband, this situation was not her intention. Then, she further explained her relationship with my husband and how she asked him several times about the status of our divorce. She started to describe my behavior referencing the six-hour flight, I discussed earlier. I interjected and caught her a bit off guard and explained to her, "adultery is adultery," and she agreed. I interjected because she does not get to interpret or dissect my feelings, nor my walk as a wife. Adultery no longer had that power. She continued, describing their time together as well as including her knowledge of my most recent schedule. This was a suitable time to end the call because the one thing I wanted to avoid with this woman, was escalation. Escalation is described as a little war (spiritual vs. earthly in this situation) that threatens to escalate into a huge ugly one. I got her attention to end the call and explained to her, "I am not sure what to tell you but to open your Bible," and I hung up. I had nothing to do with her and the situation she was in. Soon after the call, I threw my husband's cell phone out the window of the moving vehicle we road in. The phone was the only connection to her and that was my way of letting it go. Later, it dawned on me, if she had to ask my husband several times about the divorce, she knew he was married just as much as he did. It is better to walk away as Proverbs 3:35 explains, "Wise people will gain an honorable reputation, but stupid people will only add to their own disgrace." I had enough disgrace; I chose God's grace.

Chapter Four

Recovered

Recovery was like when Jesus spoke, "Peace be still," to calm the storm. The Greek defined these words "as the storm were a maniac that had to be bound and restrained," better described as a husband and wife walking in their own vision of marriage. Sometimes it is best for us to be quiet, "And the wind ceased, and there was a great calm," (Mark 4:39). This is what saved that long moment of horribleness during the ride. The call in the car was hard, but I realized those surreal moments in life are the curvy lines leading to a solid straight spiritual walk.

Writing this book was unexpected and required more of me then I envisioned. I had a friend edit the second or third version of my book and her feedback was something like this, 'You're writing listed facts, and there was nothing of you in your story.' I knew there was a deficiency in the first few versions, but I could not get my brain to work with my heart.

Emotionally, adultery was like quicksand, the more I struggled, the sand scientifically liquified, and the more trapped my legs became as the sand continued to swallow me whole. It was hard to stand still in a place filled with emotional distress. Prayer gave me peace to be still; to be a wife of God, forever holding a covenant with Him.

Prayer is what gave me hope and provided a realistic version of us. Later, my husband explained how he ended his spiritual warfare which attributed to her call. I believe this is similar to Matthew 8:28-34, when Jesus drove the demons out the man they tormented. Prayer allowed us to process the uncomfortableness of the situation and drove those demons right into a body of water as Jesus described. Patience and understanding is what changed our marriage; in 1Peter 3:7, *"Likewise, husbands, live with your wives in an understanding way, showing honor to the woman as the weaker vessel, since they are heirs with you of the grace of life, so that your prayers may not be hindered."* While we were going through adultery, my father often compared our marriage to my husband's career; explaining, he did not understand why my husband is not protecting the marriage like he protected his career, both should be an investment to a husband. Through prayer, communication, and understanding, my husband did learn to treat me as a special and fragile part of his life that should be protected to empower him. Ephesians 2:8-9: "for by grace have ye been saved through faith; and that not of yourselves, it is the gift of God; not of works, that no man should glory." We moved on from that call, one day at a time.

This next incident could be a coincidence or as in legal terms considered a 'burden of proof.' It involved an official letter from the military dated one year later from that six-hour flight, explaining to my husband, 'We are sorry to hear of the death of your spouse (my name was here). We will cancel all benefits due to the death of your spouse.' I do not know if this was a mistake or a malicious act. But anything in life that caused us to go back in time to a place our marriage should not have visited in the first place; was not God's plan for us.

We gave this moment minimum energy, realizing it was not worth risking our marital salvation. I knew I could not control the environment outside my house, but God could. I continued to talk to God to rationalize life, this ensured my marriage stayed intentional. Jesus taught in Matthew 19:6, "So they are no longer two, but one flesh. Therefore, what God has joined together, let no one separate." Each day, our love graduated to a degree not taught nor normalized in society and only known as described in His word. His type of love produced value in my marriage, my family, and my community as we worked together. Any other type of love is not of God but is an imitation from this life. The battle was never with these phone calls, this woman, or any other adulterous spirit. The battle came from us not pouring into our marriage like the Holy spirit pours into us.

Before my father-in-law passed, if I fussed about my husband, his response would be, "I gave him over to you, he is yours now." Now, I understand what he met by this. "Faith without works is dead" (James 2:17) because your belief is your behavior. Lost was who my husband was without my prayers; and highly favored was who he became as I shared in saving the best part of me. This is what saved us, making my husband's past null and void. Later, my husband explained prayer to me in his words, "You can't just pray the words to God, you have to put them into action." Flying for six hours, a family intervention, seeing me in prayer whether it was on my knees praying or praying in writing, proved who I was in this marriage, his wife. My husband nicknamed me 'Gangsta Wife,' because I was transformed. Transformed as in Romans 12:2; "Don't copy the behavior and customs of this world, but let God transform you into a new person by changing the way you think. Then you learn to know God's will for you, which is good, pleasing, and perfect." Then, my husband explained his version of love, he said, "Love was an action verb." In other words, love is not just a feeling we get to change daily, it is an activity we must pursue with intention. This is my miracle. A powerful action through God; defying common expectations in behavior with the mighty works of His power

to change the flesh, the human mind.

(5) Prayer Wall: My husband said he was happy I came to save him. God's grace and mercy is awesome. Amen

Chapter Five

Healed

Later, I told my mother this testimony, she said, "That's some story." I remember this moment at dinner, my own mother was startled and unaware of my capabilities when I was gifted God's Grace. This is why it is important for a wife to establish a healthy prayer 'wall' from day one. This is what makes her powerful as she stands beside her husband to build a family. This is how the Holy spirit works, wrapping her in the Biblical word when her better half is in need. Through prayer the Holy Spirit can hear your fears, distrust, and the animosity within your marriage. How can He help if He cannot hear your cries to Him in prayers? How will he know you? How can He keep you from harm's way if your belief in the household is divided by your own self destruction? But when you open your mind to His word, you and I can hear His answer and adhere to His obedience that stops us from becoming fools mocked by sin. Therefore, adultery never meets unforgiveness because prayer is the wall that keeps us from the other side that fills our hearts with unfulfillment. Prayer is how I gave God authority over my family. Now, when I am in my prayer room, I do not just pray, I make my prayers purposeful. This is why I shared personal prayers with my readers. First, Thessalonians 5:17 instructs us to be specific, meaningful, and consistent with God through prayer. God is always looking to guide us, especially when we are vulnerable and uncomfortable in our situations. As I look back, I know I took the long road (faithless forgiveness) to get a touch of Jesus's robe; and these are a few signals I chose to ignore:

1. I started a prayer wall but never followed through.

2. I let adultery become bigger than God.

3. As if we were center stage. Worshiping our distorted emotions is why the spirit of adultery approached, befriended, and formed a relationship within our marriage.

I know we are human, and patience is not a real virtue in most of us, so I decided to include a timeframe to represent the formula I provided earlier. My testimonial moment was in September, and we started walking in stride within our marriage in December of the same year. Three months! But when I lingered in unforgiveness, which I will now call the 'wilderness,' period (two separations). It took two years. Enough said! Do not fret about your timeframe, focus on the formula and yourself. Be aware of your own building blocks because I want you to know God's healing hand.

(6) Prayer Wall: I pray this house is our home. We remember God's humbleness and the reality that not everyone is of God but of the world. A home is about who lives in it and who prays in it. Anything else is outside noise.

I reflected on the Bible to find a good example of a woman of faith to demonstrate God's unchanging saving grace. I chose Rahab (Joshua 2). Rahab saved her family from Jericho's fate through her faith in God when she protected the two spies sent by the Israelites. A fate which resulted in the Israelites conquering Jericho and Rahab saving her family, a promise from God to his people. Jericho was a place filled with unbelievers living in sin and worshipping their own gods. Rahab gave up who she used to be because she believed in the God over the Israelites. The spies required Rahab to hang a scarlet thread from her window to remind the two spies of their promise to save her and her family in return for the sacrifice she made to save them. The spies made an oath explaining, "all your family must stay in the house, if they leave the house their blood is on their own heads. If something happens to them in the house their blood is on us." This biblical sample of family elevates how God saved then; and how he saves now. I knew my family was rescued from adultery's fate because I chose faith. The airplane ride I described earlier represented forgiveness which was my scarlet thread. A reminder of my family's worth. I see the spy's oath as a circle of protection of all those who live under the blood of Jesus. Those not wanting to stay under His protection fall to their own accountability. The Scarlet thread is my metaphor of the Christian faith in family, demonstrating protection and accountability. "Anyone who does not provide for their relatives, and especially for their own household, has denied the faith and is worse than an unbeliever," (1Timothy5:8). Who do you want to reflect?

I no longer took the journey in marriage for granted but acknowledged its inequities. I remember reading my husband's text (older text) from his friend when we first got back together. The text explained "Whatever you do, don't go back to your wife." Proof the devil's work is real and continued to try and destroy God's plan by feeding off the drama. Adultery is not God's version of marriage; divorce is not His plan for family; and both are not God's version of love. Whomever tells us different is not of God but of their own selfish imitation of love and marriage. I always complained, no one gave us a book on marriage. There was a book in my life all along, I took for granted. Now that I have picked up the Bible and dusted it off, I am filled with God's words. Jesus knew their thoughts and said to them, "Every Kingdom divided against itself will be ruined, and every city or household divided against itself will not stand. Again, be warned."

The Bible is consistent, filled with stories of flaws, sin, and so full of God's disciplinary instruction, we should use it to gain the world. The Bible shares God's redemption plan for His children, you, and me. It lays out Biblical strategy for all that we encounter. As we healed, our reality show changed into His reality and met His expectations instead of ours. This season of my marriage is healthy, stable, intimate, and exciting. Healthy, as it is safe for us to be ourselves as we reengage our marriage with a stable and safe foundation. We experience different types of intimacy; like friendships, as in retreating with other couples by talking, laughing, sharing stories, engaging in activities (shows, exercising, dancing) that inspires positive relationships. We invested in our household, by participating in Christian couple classes that brought a healthy balanced diet to our marriage. This class taught us intimacy and communication on a different level. Providing us exciting new things to try, such as hearing my husband's voice read Bible verses to me, specifically. This is hope whispering in my ears. Looking each other in the eyes each day praying for each other; and ending the prayer asking for God's forgiveness connected us spiritually. Investment is intentional, crucial, and should start from the moment we are willing and able to love someone. "Therefore, whosoever heareth these sayings of mine, and doeth them, I will liken him unto a wise man, which built his house upon a rock," (Matthew 7:24). So, I would be remiss if I did not share with you how prayer resulted in a man of God, my Husband.

Imagine if my husband did not want to save our marriage; rejected the intervention and refused to put that woman on a flight home. He could have let his pride control his faith, or embarrassment lead his heart. But he allowed the holy spirit to embrace him; this is how he fought for us, with his presence and recommitment. As you read this testimony, my husband defined love and faith in his own words through his own walk with God. This is what God does when we stop trying to control our outcome! I love my husband because of the actions he displayed in our reconciliation far out way the actions that took place in our separation. I pray my husband will continue to reach for Jesus' robe, trust Jesus' love, and know he will be blessed for his walk in Jesus. This is the answer to the formula I provided earlier. This is the outcome of a praying wife and a willing husband. I hope this seed sprouts so much that other men are open to receive the same victory to uphold their position in their marriage for their family to spread His truth.

But for now, I will share the greatest part of me, this testimony. I can tolerate the most and put up with the least. This is my providence from God. He has rescued me by putting me in a place of restoration, not only to be a woman in this world but as a prominent wife in His word. We have an unwavering firm faith and my family can receive more than we have lost in this life; because our ending is greater than our initial condition. Prayer provided faith, so forgiveness is what I decided to save myself, my husband, and my family. Now, I am blessed with moments, my husband will look me in the eyes and say, "I am glad you came to save me." This is God's work.

Dear Adultery, *God always gets the last word. You lose, as we save families one prayer wall at a time. We are humble in our victory and glorify God by making Him the center of our life! "And when you stand praying, if you hold anything against anyone, forgive them, so that your father in heaven may forgive you your sins," (Mark 11:25).*

The Prayer-Kit

Fall 2024

I really want to make sure you walk away from this book with a plan of action. Incorporate God's Word! As I discussed earlier, there is a formula to all of this - Human Conflict needs Prayer to Understand Biblical Instruction as you are reading His Word. Then this Rationalizes the Flesh to Know Discernment, resulting in Hearing the Holy Spirit (HC + P + UBI(HW)/RF + KD = HHS). In layman terms, 'this is a way to get out your mess or get out your own way.' Look at this like a toolbox that has tools with specific functions to make the motor work. But in this situation the motor is your brain, and the tools are His words so in this instance, the toolbox is a Prayer-Kit. A kit defined to equip you to conquer sin to open your pathway to victory. In this circumstance, the Prayer-Kit consists of two willing participants, a mirror, a quiet space, and a Bible to learn how to use this formula.

1. Human Conflict - Two obedient participants willing to release the past, embrace the present, and have faith in the unknown. Even if you are 10% willing to do any of these areas, this means 10% of you wants to know God. Take a chance.

2. Rationalization - A mirror is for reflection. This is where you release your flesh to allow the Holy Spirit to take over. Look in the mirror and reflect on who you were yesterday. Be honest with what you see which allows you to be honest with God. This is where the forgiveness starts with yourself, for maybe thinking you are responsible for a spouse's adultery, maybe you need more in forgiving your spouse for the adultery and forgiving the person (s) intrusive to your marriage. This opens the door to His word. Proverbs 27:17, "Intruders, as we have pointed out, are not the cause of marriage problems, but the result of the real problem."

3. Discernment - Quiet Space. Find your quiet (closet, car, park) and give some time to God - Do you know God? Are you willing to know him? Are you ready to change? Do you want to change? Are you ready to put God first? If you are willing and ready, find your space. Faithless Forgiveness vs. Faithful Forgiveness; where will your faith linger? This space is where you find out what you are really made of and who you really are in the marriage; and what you want in the marriage from your spouse. Do not be afraid, this is your space, and you are allowed to be free in it. It is important to find out who God is, was, and always will be. Take your time because He is full of patience and restoration.

4. Hearing - The Bible (includes audio version) told us Jesus already beat adultery and any sin you come against, and that means you have too. Again, the victory is yours. To be able to get to the victory,

weather you heard this before or not, you must let your flesh die; and start living through the spirit. The Bible spells it out for us. So, we must read or listen to His word to know His vision and gain His wisdom to wear His Suit of Armor. There are reading plans for the Bible where you can read or listen to the bible in 365 days. These plans help you go through the old and New Testament at the same time and keep you on track. Let the Bible keep you company while in traffic, taking a walk, or falling asleep. But whatever you do, make sure you make the moments count as part of your daily routine.

Now, put the Prayer-Kit to work! In 2Timothy 3:16-17, "All Scripture is God breathed and is useful for teaching, rebuking, correcting, and training in righteousness, so that the servant of God may be thoroughly equipped for every good work." Compare God's word, Jesus's life, and the history that encompassed it all with the present. Why? This provides facts vs. fiction like Biblical instruction vs. Worldly instruction. You will not know what I mean if you do not read for yourself. I do this a lot in my life now, and this is why I used Rahab in my book. She is a testament to what righteousness looked like then and these are the moments we should mirror. Proof that faith in God sets us apart from the rest of the world. I want to show my readers that from the beginning of time, miraculous outcomes happened when the Holy Spirit was/is involved. Let us be something new under the sun and not be a continued offender by mirroring disgrace. This chapter will be scripture focused to endorse God's word against the theatre lines you hear in this world.

The fact is the world minimizes God's thought changing miracles, divorce to not divorcing, drugs to no drugs, and so many more that we think, "Oh, look what I did." Please! People have been praying for you and me all this time. We did nothing without Him so start praising! "Look what God did for me." His word decreases those spirits from becoming a plaque that can infest the mind, marriage, and family for generations. No matter how you use the Prayer Kit, you must put God's word and promises to your life and marriage. As you are going through trials within your marriage, do not turn to the world for instruction, turn the pages of your bible and it will tell you what to do, John 14:15, "if you love Me, you will keep my commandments."

Here, God has laid down His laws and requested our obedience. Therefore, God has already proclaimed a boundary for marriage. Marriage is protected, a gift from God.

Remember, these commandments (look up 10 commandments) have not changed but only morphed to coincide with our changing world. Adultery still has consequences in a court of law. In some states it can be both a criminal offense and grounds for a fault-based divorce. As I explained earlier, we let our marriage cross boundaries. God never changed His mind on the offense.

In John 5:3, "In fact, this is love for God: to keep His commandments. And His commandments are not burdensome." God's commandments are NOT an inconvenience. The commandments are what rationalize the flesh, gives us a beginning start at life, commits us to a basic outline of His obedience to provide a peace of mind not available in this world. So, wives, we must know we are faithful women of God by showing selfless obedience to God prior and during marriage. If you made that choice to work on your marriage, there is no reason to doubt. Once you start praying to save one of God's most valuable gifts, your better half, step back, while the Holy Spirit steps in. I need to communicate; I was never angry at the physical being of adultery. I was angry at the deception in spiritual warfare, intrusion, and destruction. Again, no need to argue if you get phone calls; or invest in any confrontation because God has spoken the victory. Your faith lies in Him and not what is happening around you. Trust did not start with my husband, it started with the Holy Spirit, so do not worry about trusting your spouse right away, that will come in time. Your spouse has his own work to do with God.

In 1 John 1:9, "If we confess our sins, He is faithful and just to forgive us our sins and to cleanse us from all unrighteousness." When spouses repent, God forgives and cleanses. It says it right here in John. Husbands can regain their thrown as head of household because the Lord is faithful to His word and your spouse will be faithful to their word. In Proverbs 28:13, "Whoever conceals their sins does not prosper but the one who confesses and renounces them finds mercy." It's all here in the Bible, I am not making God's promises up. I do not have to since I have insured His word, in this testimony.

I do not claim to know all about the Bible, because I learned more and more as I wrote this book. I learned adultery can be as forgiven as in 1 John 1:7, "The blood of Jesus, God's Son, purifies us from all sin," this includes adultery. In John 8:1-11, describes how Jesus forgave an adulterous woman. While Jesus was teaching a crowd of people, the teachers of religious law approached Him with a woman who was caught in the act of adultery. In these days stoning was the consequence of adultery. The teachers asked Jesus, what they should do with the woman. And Jesus stood and said, "All right, but let the one who has never sinned throw the first stone!" One-by-one, the crowd dwindled away, until only He and the woman were left. Jesus said, "Where are your accusers? Didn't even one of them condemn you?" She said, "No, Lord." And Jesus said, "Neither do I. Go and sin no more." In His words, not mine.

Or it can be as complicated as in the life of King David. Because all sin has consequences, big or small. Read about King David in 2 Samuel 11 and learn the details of his affair with Bathsheba. It tells you about the affair, lies, deceit, murder, and consequences that resulted in spiritual blindness. Think about it this way. When you are entangled in an affair, you may feel rejuvenated, excited in the newness and ready to leave the old behind because the human flesh makes the ceremonial bliss hard, complicated, and sometimes nonnegotiable. This is what the devil does, like a thief in the night; ready to steal, kill and destroy at the first moment you argue about the bills, one spouse sleeps on the couch, or the moment you stop saying goodnight or good morning because someone did not put the laundry away. It sounds ridiculous but the devil never misses his cue, but we do. If we ever look back to where things started to fall apart in our marriage, most of us will note the most trivial thing started contention. The Bible refers to contention as linked to anger and causing fights between two people. Anger is a natural feeling but not met to be an action verb so stop making it an active (like we did) part of your marriage but leave it as a feeling to reflect and observe its source. You know what I just did, rationalized my thoughts through discernment. Not too bad for a late bloomer of His word.

I want you to see the war is real and compare it to your life or surroundings. Take heed but do not judge those relationships that do not put God first, pray for them instead. I want you to know that there is someone fighting for you, but you must be willing to do your homework to find out more about Him. In 1John 3:8, "The reason the Son of God appeared was to destroy the devil's work." In the words of Jesus Christ as He described the devil to the non-believers in John 8:44, "You belong to your father, the devil, and you want to carry out your father's desires. He was a murderer from the beginning, not holding to the truth, for there is no truth in him. When he lies, he speaks his native language, for he is a liar and the father of lies." Stay away from the devil's work and become familiar with his way so you can see through and around it. We all live under one God, who cherishes what He puts together in love, peace, and harmony so why would He want His creation to end in disaster.

The good news is just as the Bible gives us laws with consequences; it gives accolades to those who build His kingdom by embracing and adopting His commandments. God provides His intentions for marriage and the joyous praises the union of husband and wife provides to the heavens. This includes what He wants us to get from marriage, "Let your fountain be blessed and rejoice in the wife of your youth" (Proverbs 5:18). "Let marriage be held in honor among all and let the marriage bed be undefiled" (Hebrews 13:4). Undefiled means to keep the bedroom clean and pure from fornication, adultery, homosexuality, prostitution, and pornography and anything else the Bible finds unpure. So, outside of the impureness, a couple is open to fulfill this department in marriage to their satisfaction, Enjoy! 1 Corinthians 7:2-5: "Each man should have sexual relations with his own wife, and each woman with her own husband. The husband should fulfill his marital duty to his wife, and likewise the wife to her husband." Nothing in this says things should be one sided. In 1Corinthians 7:3-5 says "that, for a limited time, spouses may agree to not have sex to devote themselves more fully to prayer. Then come together again so that Satan will not tempt you because of your lack of self-control." Notice it says come together again, even God knows the flesh. He created us, enjoy His pleasures.

Everything is owed to God, "For from him and through him and to him are all things. To him be the glory forever. Amen" (Romans 11:36). "In order that in everything God may be glorified through Jesus Christ" (1 Peter 4:11). This is the goal of everything, including marriage. Do not worry about where your relationship is going with your spouse; you both need to focus on where your relationship is with God. Because once you have His forgiveness both of you will move towards a common goal to forgive each other. I will end with, if you can learn to truly put the Prayer-Kit to work like your life depends on it, because it does, you will know Joshua 1:8 NIV, "keep this Book of the Law always on your lips; meditate on it day and night, so that you may be careful to do everything written in it. Then you will be prosperous and successful." God has spoken, welcome to your victory!

(7) Prayer Wall: The faith of one person in the household can change your entire family. Amen

Journal

Tell Your Story

Learn who God is through the Prayer-Kit and start your new walk in Christ.

_____

_____

_____

_____

_____

_____

_____

_____

_____

_____

_____

_____